TURNING POINTS

THE 9/11 ATTACKS

BY LAURA K. MURRAY

CREATIVE EDUCATION • CREATIVE PAPERBACKS

Published by Creative Education and Creative Paperbacks
P.O. Box 227, Mankato, Minnesota 56002
Creative Education and Creative Paperbacks are imprints of
The Creative Company
www.thecreativecompany.us

Design and production by The Design Lab
Art direction by Rita Marshall
Printed in China

Photographs by Corbis (Diane Bondareff/epa, Ken Cedeno, GERADO
MAGALLON/Reuters, Reuters, Ron Sachs/CNP, Ron Sachs/CNP/Sygma, Ruet
Stephane, STR/Reuters, JIM YOUNG/Reuters), Creative Commons Wikimedia
(Nightscream), Dreamstime (Georgios Kollidas), Getty Images (AFP, AFP/
Ahmed Al-Rubaye, AFP PHOTO/Staff, Spencer Platt, Mario Tama, USAF, Syed
Zargham), NASA (NASA), Shutterstock (L. Kragt Bakker, Larry Bruce, Songquan
Deng, Jesse Kunerth, Sean Pavone)

Library of Congress Cataloging-in-Publication Data
Murray, Laura K.
The 9/11 attacks / Laura K. Murray.
p. cm. — (Turning points)
Includes bibliographical references and index.
Summary: A historical account of the 9/11 terrorist attacks, including the
events leading up to that day, the people involved, the monumental rescue and
recovery efforts, and the lingering aftermath.

ISBN 978-1-60818-750-8 (hardcover)
ISBN 978-1-62832-346-7 (pbk)
ISBN 978-1-56660-785-8 (eBook)
September 11 Terrorist Attacks, 2001—Juvenile literature.

HV6432.7.M88 2016
973.931—dc23   2016002146

CCSS: RI.5.1, 2, 3, 8; RI. 6.1, 2, 4, 7; RH.6-8.3, 4, 5, 6, 7, 8

First Edition HC 9 8 7 6 5 4 3 2 1
First Edition PBK 9 8 7 6 5 4 3 2 1

Cover, main image, and this page: The annual Tribute in Light art
installation of 88 searchlights, remembering the events of September 11

TABLE *of* CONTENTS

INTRODUCTION

As the 21st century dawned, the United States was arguably the most powerful nation on Earth. Since emerging from World War II as a superpower, the U.S. had involved itself in many other countries' affairs. But such actions had fueled frustration and resentment in places around the world. In the Middle East, a growing movement of Islamic **extremism** viewed the U.S. as its main enemy. Two symbols of American **economic** power and influence became targets to destroy.

Completed in 1973, New York's World Trade Center (WTC) was renowned for its 110-story "Twin Towers" that arose from the Manhattan skyline. The north and south towers were part of a seven-building complex. Each day, as many as 50,000 people worked in the towers' banks, restaurants, and offices, while thousands more visited.

On September 11, 2001, terrorists hijacked four U.S. passenger airplanes. They crashed the planes into the Twin Towers, the **Pentagon** in Washington, D.C., and a Pennsylvania field. Nearly 3,000 were killed, and cleanup efforts lasted nearly 2 years.

The 9/11 attacks altered American attitudes, government, and politics. Soon, the U.S. found itself embroiled in a global War on Terror against an elusive enemy. As it turned out, this age of terrorism had been escalating for many years.

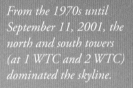

From the 1970s until September 11, 2001, the north and south towers (at 1 WTC and 2 WTC) dominated the skyline.

Using their holiest book as a weapon against other religions is not a trait restricted to adherents of extremist Islam.

CHAPTER ONE

THE BASE

In 1980, 23-year-old Osama bin Laden arrived in Afghanistan. The Saudi Arabian university graduate had come to help the Afghan **resistance** force, known as the mujahideen. The rebels were fighting off an invasion from the Soviet Union. Using his family fortune, bin Laden helped set up a network of contacts for donations, recruitment, and training. The U.S. was also secretly funding the mujahideen against the **communist** Soviets.

Bin Laden and other foreign fighters were part of a **fundamentalist** Islamic movement. They wanted to wage jihad (holy war) against non-religious governments of Muslim countries. Bin Laden and other followers thought of themselves as heroic, holy warriors who would be rewarded after death. By 1988, the Soviets had been defeated. But bin Laden and his followers wanted to keep running their network. Around this time, they named the organization al Qaeda ("the base") and planned to take jihad to other parts of the world. According to Abdullah Azzam, an al Qaeda founder, jihad would be necessary "until all other lands that were Muslim are returned to us, so that Islam will rule again."

Osama bin Laden

Radical movements such as al Qaeda continued to grow. Afghanistan and Pakistan became training grounds for young militants. The volunteers learned how to fire guns and make bombs. They also were taught about the perceived struggle of Islam against the West (places such as Europe and North America). According to a 2010 report by Colonel John M. Venhaus, most young al Qaeda recruits came from relatively normal backgrounds—with little formal understanding of Islamic teachings. Struggling with identity and purpose, they became vulnerable to al Qaeda's messages. "Al Qaeda has spent years promoting and perfecting its brand management strategy to appear to young Muslims as if it were the only answer to all their problems," Venhaus said.

Al Qaeda and other extremists soon singled out the U.S. as the main enemy, "the head of the

POINTING OUT

UNDERSTANDING ISLAM

*With an estimated 1.6 billion Muslims around the world, Islam is the world's second-largest religion (after Christianity). Like Christians and Jews, Muslims believe there is one God, called Allah. Allah's words to the prophet Muhammad make up Islam's holy book, the Qur'an (Koran). Muslims follow the Five Pillars of Islam: faith, worship, charity, fasting, and **pilgrimage**. As with any religion, extremists do not represent the beliefs of most Muslims. "It's not courageous to attack innocent children, women, and civilians. It's courageous to protect freedom," said Egyptian Islamic cleric Sheikh Mohammed Sayed Tantawi after 9/11. More than a decade later, terror groups continued acting in the name of Islam.*

Burning a flag may be an expression of free speech in the U.S., but when done elsewhere, it takes on a different tone.

snake." They said the U.S. was evil, non-religious, power-hungry—and the source of all Muslim conflict. They opposed the U.S.'s military presence and cultural influence in the Middle East (particularly Saudi Arabia) and among its holy sites. They were also angered by U.S. support of Israel. Jews, American allies, and even other Muslims were labeled enemies as well. Matters were complicated further by the long-standing history of conflict among Muslims, Christians, and Jews—as well as U.S. dependence on Middle Eastern oil.

Some terrorists were ready to take their war to American soil. On February 26, 1993, a Pakistani man named Ramzi Yousef and a partner drove a van into the parking garage below New York's World Trade Center. The van was loaded with a bomb. When the vehicle exploded minutes later, it blasted a 200-foot-wide (61 m) crater through the concrete. It knocked out electricity, cut water pipes, gushed smoke and fire, and sent heavy steel shooting through the air. Six people were killed, while another 1,042 were wounded. After his arrest two years later, Yousef said his group had been trying to bring one tower crashing into the other.

Bin Laden wasn't directly involved in the WTC bombing, but Yousef had trained at an al Qaeda camp. Over the next few years, bin Laden continued to provide money, weapons, and training for terror activities around the globe. He also made alliances with other groups against the U.S.

One of those alliances was with the Taliban. After taking over war-torn Afghanistan in 1996, the Taliban enforced harsh laws to return the country to "pure" Islam. The group outlawed laughing in public, dancing, non-religious music, photography, television, paintings, and even stuffed animals. Men were required to cut their hair and grow beards. Women, who suffered the most severely, were forced to cover their faces and bodies and were banned from attending work or school. The Taliban gladly gave bin Laden refuge in 1996 after he had been kicked out of both Saudi Arabia and Sudan. From that year until 2001, bin Laden's terror camps trained an estimated 10,000 to 20,000 fighters.

Ayman al-Zawahiri

On August 23, 1996, bin Laden issued a declaration of war against the U.S. "Muslims burn with anger at America," it said. The declaration called for attacks against U.S. troops stationed in the Persian Gulf. Then, in 1998, bin Laden joined with Egyptian terrorist leader Ayman al-Zawahiri to issue another declaration of war. This one stated, "To kill Americans and their allies—civilians and military—is an individual duty for every Muslim who can do it in any country in which it is possible to do it."

Violence soon followed. On August 7, 1998, U.S. embassies in Kenya and Tanzania were bombed. Nearly 250 people were killed (including 12 Americans), and more than 4,500 were injured. Under president Bill Clinton, the U.S. responded with missile strikes against suspected terror bases in Afghanistan and Sudan.

Over the next few years, the U.S. made formal accusations against bin Laden and al Qaeda. They were charged with **conspiring** to kill Americans, as well as with masterminding the embassy bombings and the deadly 2000 attack

In Nairobi, Kenya, the 1998 embassy bombing affected nearby buildings and incinerated two passing buses.

The attack on the USS Cole *occurred as the crew of 293 were lining up for lunch in the ship's galley, or kitchen.*

on the USS *Cole*. Soon after, a *Newsweek* article called the U.S. "woefully unprepared" to handle terror attacks. Bin Laden—by now, one of the Federal Bureau of Investigation (FBI)'s most-wanted criminals—willingly participated in media interviews. "Hostility toward America is a religious duty, and we hope to be rewarded for it by God," he told *TIME* magazine.

Terrorists had long been thinking about how to stage a bigger kind of attack. Khalid Sheikh Mohammed (known as "KSM") had a plan: he wanted to attack the U.S. using commercial airplanes. After KSM joined al Qaeda, bin Laden agreed to finance the plot in 1999. By this time,

POINTING OUT

TERROR AT SEA

In 2000, al Qaeda upped its attacks against U.S. forces. On October 12, the U.S. Navy destroyer USS Cole *was refueling in Yemen when terrorists detonated a bomb in a small boat alongside it. The explosion blasted a 40-foot-wide (12.2 m) hole in the navy ship. Seventeen sailors were killed, and about 40 were injured. Bin Laden later took credit for the attack and even wrote a poem about it. According to bin Laden, "The destroyer represented the capital of the West, and the small boat represented Muhammad." Al Qaeda used the attack to bolster its recruitment efforts.*

The hijackers involved in the WTC attacks would soon be identified; the top line shows suspects on United Airlines Flight 175, and the bottom line pictures those aboard American Airlines Flight 11.

al Qaeda had an estimated yearly budget of $30 million. Bin Laden eventually approved four targets: the Pentagon, the World Trade Center, and possibly the U.S. Capitol or White House in Washingon, D.C.

The next step was choosing the men to carry out the suicide missions. Egyptian Mohamed Atta became the leader of the hijackers. He and three others would fly the aircraft. Fifteen more hijackers, most from Saudi Arabia, would serve as the "muscle." They were to control the pilots, passengers, and crew.

KSM helped train the team and teach them about Western culture. The men shaved their beards and uncovered their heads to blend in with Americans. They rented cars and joined gyms. A few attended flight school. By the summer of 2001, all the hijackers were in the U.S. and stationed near East Coast airports. On the night of September 10, the hijackers received their final instructions (likely from Atta): "when the time of truth comes and the Zero Hour arrives, ... embrace death for the sake of Allah!" The terror of the next morning would change the world forever.

CHAPTER TWO

102 MINUTES

On Tuesday, September 11, 2001, the morning sky above Manhattan was blue and clear. New York City's polls were open for **primary** elections. School was in session like any other weekday. People were arriving to work, including those employed at businesses located in the World Trade Center. About 17,500 people would be in the Twin Towers by 8:45 A.M.

Early that morning, the 19 hijackers each cleared airport security—despite several being chosen for additional screening. At 7:59 A.M., American Airlines Flight 11 took off from Boston's Logan International Airport. It was bound for Los Angeles and carried 76 passengers, 11 crew members, and 5 hijackers. Fifteen minutes into the flight, the hijackers took over the plane. One hijacker (possibly Atta) accidentally contacted ground control rather than the passengers in the cabin. "We have some planes," he said. "Just stay quiet, and you will be okay. We are returning to the airport." Instead, the plane turned toward New York City. Around the same time, United Airlines Flight 175 took off from Logan, also headed for Los Angeles.

At 8:19 A.M., Betty Ong, a flight attendant aboard Flight 11, used a phone in the back of the plane to report the hijacking. In a separate call, flight attendant Madeline "Amy" Sweeney said that hijackers had stabbed two flight attendants and a passenger. The hijackers had used a type of pepper spray and claimed to have a bomb. The information provided by Sweeney and Ong—including the hijackers'

Madeline "Amy" Sweeney

seat numbers—would later prove to be essential in piecing together the day's events.

As Flight 11 was being hijacked, another plane was taking off. American Airlines Flight 77 left Washington Dulles International Airport for Los Angeles at 8:14 A.M. Thirty-two minutes later, the delayed United Airlines Flight 93 took off from New Jersey's Newark International Airport, bound for San Francisco. All four targeted planes were now in the air.

On board Flight 11, Sweeney reported seeing water and buildings. At 8:46 A.M., the plane slammed into the north tower of the World Trade Center. It plowed through the 93rd through 99th floors, killing everyone on board and hundreds more inside the tower. The plane's 10,000 gallons (37,854 l) of jet fuel exploded into fire and billowing smoke.

Within minutes of the crash, members of the Fire Department of New York (FDNY) and the New York Police Department (NYPD) arrived at the scene. Loaded down with equipment, they ran into the tower as confused—but mostly calm—workers filed out. The **Port Authority of New York and New Jersey** tried to help evacuate the building. But the tower's emergency stairwells had been destroyed, trapping those who worked above the impact zone. Many fell to their deaths trying to escape the choking smoke and fire. Others jumped. Workers in the south tower were initially told to stay put. Many ignored the warning and escaped to safety.

Smoke billowed from the north tower from Flight 11's impact as Flight 175 struck the south tower 17 minutes later.

Meanwhile, media had arrived to investigate. "My heavens…. It appears, at least from this vantage point, that something has hit [the north tower]," said radio traffic reporter Tom Kaminski. Breaking news bulletins took over programming, showing live images of the raging fire. "We have no idea if it was a plane," said ABC's Diane Sawyer. "Was it in any sense deliberate? Was it an accident?"

It soon became clear that it was no accident. Passengers of Flight 175 were also reporting their plane had been hijacked. At 9:03 A.M., millions of television viewers watched in horror as that

POINTING OUT

ESCAPING ALIVE

Although thousands lost their lives on 9/11, others amazingly survived—often with the help of strangers. After the first plane hit, window washer Jan Demczur and 5 others became stuck in an elevator at the WTC north tower's 50th floor. They pried open the door and then used Demczur's brass squeegee handle to cut through a wall and escape. In another incident, Port Authority officers Will Jimeno and John McLoughlin were buried beneath the rubble for 13 and 22 hours respectively before being rescued. McLoughlin, who was severely injured, later said, "Nobody will ever fully recover from what happened that day."

Observers on the ground a few blocks away from the WTC stood in shock and horror as they witnessed the unthinkable.

NO STANDING

7AM – 7PM
MON – FRI
EXCEPT
AUTHORIZED
VEHICLES
←

DEPT. OF
CORRECTIONS
VEHICLES

plane appeared on their screens. It banked and crashed into the south tower at 587 miles (945 km) per hour. The impact killed the 64 aboard and hundreds inside the building. As in the north tower, many of the building's escape routes were blocked or doors jammed. Some called 9-1-1 to find out what was going on. But they often heard busy signals or received inaccurate information from overwhelmed operators.

Only a handful of people above the impact zone—floors 77 through 85—managed to escape using a stairwell. Brian Clark worked in a brokerage firm on the 84th floor. "We didn't know anything other than suddenly we were in chaos and our building had been hit," he recalled. He and a few others wrestled their way through debris and darkened passages full of sloshing water to reach the street level.

There they encountered a chaotic scene. The NYPD had sent out more than 2,000 responders, while the FDNY had called in more than 230 firefighters. Medical personnel, off-duty police and firefighters, and other volunteers also arrived to help. A command center was set up in the north tower lobby. Across the country, people in homes, businesses, and schools were watching in disbelief as the events unfolded on live TV.

George W. Bush

By this time, president George W. Bush, who had been visiting a Florida elementary school, had been alerted. But authorities had not been prepared for such a large-scale attack. After the first hijacking, North American Aerospace Defense Command (NORAD) had sent out a few fighter jets, but they were too far away to help. Muddled communications with the Federal Aviation Administration (FAA) added to the confusion.

Officials then received word that a third plane had been hijacked. At 9:37 A.M., Flight 77 crashed into the west wall of the Pentagon, exploding into a 300-foot (91.4 m) fireball. All 59 aboard were killed, in addition to 125 inside the damaged building. With the nation now definitively under attack, all U.S. flights were grounded. Inbound international flights were redirected to Canada or Mexico. The White House, Capitol, and other government buildings were evacuated throughout the morning.

Then, just before 10:00 A.M., another unthinkable event happened. The WTC's weakened south tower collapsed in just 10 seconds, burying hundreds inside. Splintered debris rained down, and a giant, tornado-like cloud of burning ash and dust rose into the air. People on the street scrambled for cover. "Everybody looked up, and, as in a disaster movie, everybody started running," Clark said.

As the south tower crumbled, passengers and crew aboard Flight 93 were fighting back against the hijackers. At 10:03 A.M., the aircraft slammed into a field in Shanksville,

It took five weeks of 24/7 work to clean up and restore millions of square feet of office space at the damaged Pentagon.

Pennsylvania, killing all 44 aboard. The plane was only 20 minutes' flying time from Washington, D.C. Soon after, the Pentagon's damaged wall collapsed.

Back in New York, rescue units were told to evacuate the north tower. But many firefighters didn't receive the orders because of confusion or faulty radio communications. At 10:28 A.M., 102 minutes after the crash of Flight 11, the north tower collapsed. More than 1,400 people were still inside. When the dust settled, both towers were gone. In their place was a mountain of mangled debris. Under a gray sky, white ash descended upon the streets like snow.

POINTING OUT

FIGHTING FOR FLIGHT 93

On the hijacked United Airlines Flight 93, passengers and crew learned about the attacks in New York and Washington. After a vote, they decided to take back control of the plane. Some even boiled water to throw at the hijackers. Then an operator on the line with passenger Todd Beamer heard him say, "Let's roll." Over the phone, flight attendant Sandra Bradshaw told her husband, "Everyone's running up to first class. I've got to go. Bye." As passengers stormed the cockpit, the hijackers rolled and pitched the plane to throw them off. Recovered flight recordings relay sounds of struggle as well as the hijackers' yells to each other to crash the plane.

CHAPTER THREE

RESCUE AND RECOVERY

After the north tower's collapse, New York mayor Rudolph Giuliani ordered the evacuation of Lower Manhattan. People left the city on foot, weaving their way through ash-covered streets and crossing bridges in large crowds. Others were taken by boat, staring back at the skyline in shock. But rescue workers continued arriving. Firefighters tried to combat the blazes that cropped up. Together with police, dogs, and other workers, they searched for survivors in the rubble. At 5:20 P.M., the evacuated 47-story building at 7 WTC collapsed after burning for hours.

The constant media coverage continued. It replaced regular programming on networks throughout the country, replaying the crashes and aftermath over and over. Confusion and rumors sometimes led to false alarms and inaccurate reports, including one of a car bombing. Many worried that a second wave of attacks was coming. Even as facts slowly came in, though, officials had already zeroed in on al Qaeda and identified all 19 hijackers. (Bin Laden would not admit the organization's involvement until 2004.)

New York first responder

*Newspapers in other cities printed extra editions
of their daily papers after the attacks.*

On the evening of September 11, President Bush addressed the nation. "Today, our fellow citizens, our way of life, our very freedom came under attack in a series of deliberate and deadly terrorist acts," he said. "A great people has been moved to defend a great nation. Terrorist attacks can shake the foundations of our biggest buildings, but they cannot touch the foundation of America." Bush then focused on those responsible. "We will make no distinction between the terrorists who committed these acts and those who harbor them," he said. "We stand together to win the war against terrorism."

Across the nation, people tried to make sense of what had happened. In New York, photos covered lampposts and buildings as families searched for information on missing loved ones. Volunteers arrived at the crash sites as efforts continued around the clock. One electrician set up cables and movie lights to help with the search. "It was my duty as a human being—an American—and a New Yorker to be there," he said. Others donated blood or gave money to relief funds. Sporting and entertainment events were canceled. The stock market remained closed until September 17. Everywhere, people mourned those killed, holding vigils and prayer services.

Feelings of patriotism soared. Stores quickly sold out of American flags. Many Americans felt more united and compassionate toward one

The term "ground zero" refers to a site of devastation and soon became synonymous with the area around the WTC.

another. However, the friendly feelings did not always extend to everyone. Some people blamed all Muslims for the terror attacks. Muslim Americans sometimes became the victims of harassment, threats, and violence. People of Middle Eastern descent were also targeted, as were Sikhs (who wear turbans and beards as part of their religion). In reality, the majority of Muslim leaders denounced the attacks. Salih bin Muhammad Al-Luehidan, chairman of the Supreme Judicial Council of Saudi Arabia, called the 9/11 terrorists "the worst of people.... Anyone who thinks that any Islamic scholar will condone such acts is totally wrong."

POINTING OUT

CROSS CONTROVERSY

*Days after 9/11, a cleanup worker uncovered two intersecting steel beams in the WTC rubble. Workers, families, and, later, tourists flocked to the 17-foot (5.2 m) cross. In 2011, the National September 11 Memorial & Museum installed the cross as part of its display. American **Atheists** Inc. filed a lawsuit to remove it. But the museum stated that the cross was important history. "It provided comfort to ... people who were working in some of the most hellish conditions imaginable," said museum president and chief executive Joseph C. Daniels. In 2014, a judge dismissed the lawsuit, and an appeals court upheld the decision.*

Photos of the missing and memorials to the victims of 9/11 appeared around New York in the days after the attacks.

For the most part, the global community responded in solidarity with the U.S. In London, "The Star-Spangled Banner" played during Buckingham Palace's Changing of the Guard. In places as far away as Iran, schools and stadiums held moments of silence. Church bells in Europe chimed. Polish firefighters sounded their sirens. The front page of the French newspaper *Le Monde* read, "*Nous sommes tous Américains*" (We are all Americans). From **dictators** to the pope, world leaders condemned the attacks. Other **North Atlantic Treaty Organization (NATO)** countries announced that they viewed the attack as an attack on all of them—and would fight with the U.S.

Citizens of some countries were unsympathetic, though. Videos surfaced of street crowds in Pakistan burning American flags and celebrating Americans' deaths. From Iraq, **Saddam Hussein** expressed support of the attacks.

Back in the U.S., search-and-rescue teams found very few survivors. At 12:30 P.M. on September 12, Port Authority secretary Genelle Guzman-McMillan was rescued from the wreckage of the north tower. She was the last person pulled out alive, although searches continued for weeks.

On October 6, New York's operation officially shifted to recovery. The media had dubbed the World Trade Center site as "Ground Zero," but workers called it simply "The Pile." Besides concrete and glass, the smoldering Pile also contained human remains. DNA testing helped identify many victims, but around 41 percent of those missing would remain unidentified more than a decade later. Relief workers contended with dangerous conditions, long hours, and ongoing health issues from inhaling dust and toxins. Each time a body was found, all work stopped as a final sign of respect. The death toll reached 2,973—the largest-ever loss of life from an

Dangerous conditions prompted New York City officials to scale back the presence of uniformed personnel by November 2001.

attack on American soil. The number included 343 from the FDNY, 37 from the Port Authority, and 23 from the NYPD.

Cleanup operations were also underway at the three attack sites. At Ground Zero, construction professionals, engineers, firefighters, and volunteers labored to clear the approximately 1.8 million tons (1.6 t) of debris. Relief stations provided workers with food, medical care, and other support. Federal agents and others then sorted through the debris piece by piece off-site. Official cleanup efforts would continue until May 2002, at a cost of about $750 million.

Meanwhile, government agencies were investigating the attacks.

The federal government soon offered a $25-million reward for information leading to the capture of bin Laden.

Thousands of FBI agents swarmed the crash sites, interviewing witnesses, taking photographs, and collecting evidence. Deep in the Pennsylvania crater, they located Flight 93's cockpit voice recorder and flight data recorder. Recorders were also found at the Pentagon.

On September 20, 2001, President Bush addressed a joint session of Congress, calling for the capture of those responsible. "Our War on Terror begins with al Qaeda, but it does not end there," he said. "It will not end until every terrorist group of global reach has been found, stopped, and defeated." Then he gave the Taliban a five-part **ultimatum**. If the organization did not turn over al Qaeda leaders, Afghanistan would be invaded. Bush also called on other countries to support the War on Terror. "Every nation in every region now has a decision to make," he said. "Either you are with us, or you are with the terrorists."

The U.S. rejected the Taliban's attempts to negotiate. On October 7, the U.S. launched Operation Enduring Freedom by invading Afghanistan. Joined by Afghan rebels and countries such as Great Britain, U.S. forces bombed Taliban and al Qaeda targets. By 2002, the Taliban had been ousted from power, but bin Laden and other terrorists had escaped. The global War on Terror was just beginning.

POINTING OUT

TERRORISTS AS PRISONERS

In January 2002, the U.S. government opened the Guantánamo Bay detention camp in Cuba. The military prison held suspected terrorists without trial. Calls to close the camp increased with allegations of prisoner abuse and torture. Still, leaders remained at odds over what to do with the prisoners. The matter was compounded when the U.S. was found to have committed shocking human rights abuses against prisoners at an Iraqi prison. During the 2008 presidential campaign, Barack Obama pledged to close Guantánamo within the first year of his presidency. As of 2015, 132 detainees remained at the camp.

Afghan fighters who opposed the Taliban's influence in their country helped the U.S. capture al Qaeda operatives.

CHAPTER FOUR

A NEW KIND OF WAR

Even as people in Afghanistan enjoyed new freedoms, the War on Terror earned many critics in the U.S. and abroad. Some accused the Bush administration of using 9/11 as an excuse to invade countries and use **preemptive** strikes. Others were concerned that there could be no clear winner—or end—to a war against terrorism. And in this case, the enemy had no regard for human life. "The Americans love Pepsi Cola; we love death," said al Qaeda spokesman Maulana Inyadullah.

A U.S.-led **coalition** trained Afghan police forces and worked to rebuild the country's government. But the Taliban reorganized in 2003 and continued to wage bloody attacks. That same year, the U.S. invaded Iraq, which it had labeled as part of the "**Axis of Evil**." Operation Iraqi Freedom deposed dictator Saddam Hussein, but violent civil war erupted soon after. The Iraq War was not popular among U.S. allies.

In a single day, life at home had changed as well. "We're learning once again that freedom and liberty and the American way of life are not a birthright," said secretary of the navy Gordon England. And

Saddam Hussein

Four years into the Iraq War,
Americans who wanted peace
continued to demonstrate in the
nation's capital.

The anthrax attack killed two postal workers, causing employees of the Postal Service to be wary when handling mail.

new threats were surfacing. Soon after 9/11, five people died after coming into contact with mailed letters containing strains of the anthrax disease. The case awakened Americans to the potential for **biological attacks**. Then, in December, a man on a flight to the U.S. unsuccessfully attempted to light explosives hidden in the soles of his shoes.

According to a 2010 *Washington Post* report, at least 263 government organizations were created or reorganized in the wake of 9/11. The Aviation and Transportation Security Act of 2001 put airport security under federal control. It created the Transportation Security Administration (TSA). The TSA's new security measures included passenger screening and strict carry-on restrictions. But critics accused the organization of invading privacy and being ineffective. On October 8, 2001, President Bush signed an executive order establishing the Office of Homeland Security. It was restructured as the Department of Homeland Security in November 2002. It focused on protecting the U.S. through border, aviation, and cyber security as well as emergency response. Some existing agencies, such as the FBI, shifted their priorities to better combat advanced forms of terrorism such as **cyberterrorism**.

New policies spurred debate. The USA PATRIOT Act of 2001 granted the government more power to perform phone and computer tapping, conduct searches, and access private records. Under the authority of the Patriot Act, the National Security Agency (NSA) began tracking huge amounts of communications worldwide. Both the act and the NSA soon came under fire and were accused of overstepping their bounds. With parts of the Patriot Act set to expire in June 2015, Congress continued debating surveillance reforms.

In the days and years following September 11th, a question haunted everyone: why had the U.S. failed to prevent the attacks? From Clinton and Bush to the Central Intelligence Agency (CIA) and FBI, leaders and agencies came under scrutiny. So-called "9/11 Truthers" believed the events were the results of a government conspiracy or cover-up.

To address these questions, in 2002, President Bush created the National Commission on Terrorist Attacks upon the United States. The 9/11 Commission, as it became known, was made up of five Republicans and five Democrats. They were responsible for not only investigating 9/11 but also recommending how to prevent future attacks. The Commission pored over millions of pages of information and interviewed more than 1,200 people. In addition, the Commission studied airport security footage and audio from the recovered flight data recorders.

The Commission released its final report in July 2004. "Across the government, there were failures of imagination, policies, capabilities, and management," it concluded. "Al Qaeda's new brand of terrorism presented challenges to the U.S. governmental institutions that they were not well-designed to meet." The report listed numerous recommendations to have intelligence agencies work together to combat terrorism, especially in vulnerable areas such as border and

Until the 9/11 Commission delivered its final report, it continued to hear testimony from people with privileged information.

Those who lost loved ones to combat in Iraq and Afghanistan paid a high personal price in the War on Terror.

immigration security. Those issues would remain hotly debated topics throughout the next decade.

President Bush's approval rating, which had skyrocketed to 90 percent in the weeks after 9/11, steadily declined as foreign wars dragged on. His narrow reelection in 2004 showed a deeply divided country. When the Iraq War officially ended in 2011, more than 4,400 U.S. troops had been killed, and violence between Iraqis continued. In December 2014, U.S. forces ended combat operations in Afghanistan. More than 2,200 U.S. soldiers had been killed there since the war's start.

Meanwhile, the worldwide hunt for terrorists continued. In November 2001, the U.S. killed al

POINTING OUT

KILLING BIN LADEN

Early on May 2, 2011, SEAL Team Six stormed a compound in Abbottabad, Pakistan. The 38-minute raid killed Osama bin Laden and 4 others. Bin Laden's body was transported to a U.S. aircraft carrier and then buried at sea. That evening, President Obama addressed the nation. "The death of bin Laden marks the most significant achievement to date in our nation's effort to defeat al Qaeda," he said. Across the country, celebrations broke out. The U.S. had come close to killing the terrorist leader several times before. This time, Americans had used remote-controlled drone aircraft to track bin Laden for months prior to the raid.

Crowds gathered outside the White House as President Obama told the nation of bin Laden's death in 2011.

Qaeda's military chief, Mohammed Atef, in an air strike. In March 2003, KSM (widely considered the "architect" of 9/11) was captured in Pakistan. He and other terrorists were sent to Guantánamo Bay detention camp in Cuba. Abu Musab al-Zarqawi, the leader of al Qaeda in Iraq, was killed in 2006 by a U.S. air strike. And in 2011, U.S. special forces took out bin Laden, finally ending a decade-long manhunt.

But even as the U.S. eliminated individual terrorists, other groups were gaining power. In 2014, the jihadist group sometimes known as ISIL (*EYE-sil*) or ISIS (*EYE-sis*) took over parts of Iraq and Syria. The group began calling itself the Islamic State (IS). The extremists recruited thousands of fighters with the goal of establishing fundamentalist **sharia** law in the Middle East. Governments the world over decried the organization's kidnappings, murders, and other crimes. The U.S. began taking military action against IS in mid-2014.

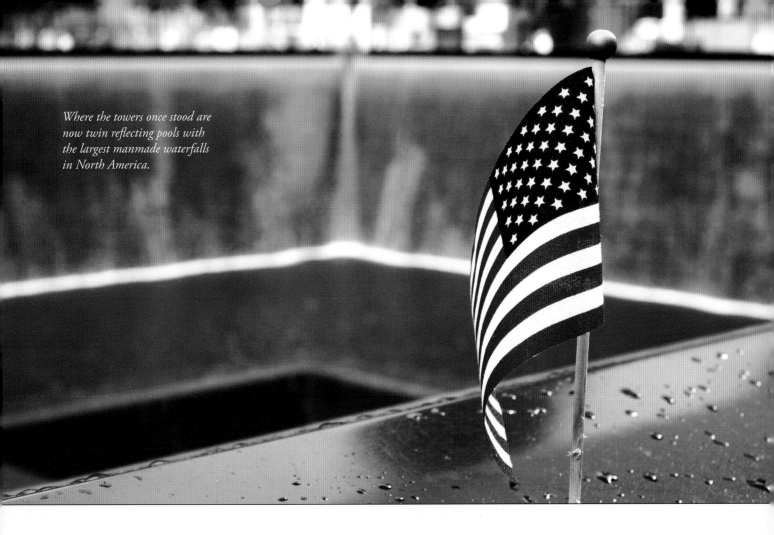

Where the towers once stood are now twin reflecting pools with the largest manmade waterfalls in North America.

A 2011 estimate put 9/11's costs to the U.S. at $3.3 trillion. But the human toll was much greater. Memorials around the country stand in remembrance of the victims. In Pennsylvania, the outdoor Flight 93 National Memorial features a wall of names. The Pentagon Memorial contains 184 benches, 1 for each victim. In 2011, the National September 11 Memorial & Museum opened where the Twin Towers once stood. Rebuilding was also taking place nearby. Completed in 2014, One World Trade Center stood 1,776 feet (541 m) high, a nod to the year of America's independence. The 104-story tower housed offices and an observatory.

Even as life moved on, the legacy of 9/11 remained—and new questions arose. In early 2015, testimony from convicted 9/11 plotter Zacarias Moussaoui caused some to wonder if other countries had funded al Qaeda before the attacks. That same year, an independent, congressionally mandated panel issued

Beams of light representing the Twin Towers memorialize the day that has become a symbol of national resilience.

POINTING OUT

AN ONGOING THREAT

After 9/11, other countries also experienced coordinated terror attacks. On March 11, 2004, terrorists targeted four crowded trains in Madrid, Spain. Then, on July 7, 2005, bombers set off explosives in London's subway system and on a bus. "It was an indiscriminate attempt to slaughter, [without] any considerations for age, for class, for religion, or whatever," said Metropolitan police commissioner Sir Ian Blair. In 2015, an Israeli study found that suicide attacks had doubled worldwide in 2014, particularly in the Middle East. According to the study, this was caused by government instability in the Middle East, the rise of ISIS, and the U.S. withdrawal from Afghanistan.

a largely positive review of the FBI's progress since the 9/11 Commission Report. The review stated that the FBI had "transformed itself over the last 10 years." It also included recommendations for the agency as it worked to stay ahead of new threats.

When Americans woke up on September 12, 2001, life was different. The 9/11 terror attacks challenged views on safety, war, immigration, government, torture, privacy, and religion. They led to wars and other military actions that continue today. But they also showed how Americans are capable of uniting in the face of tragedy. People will never forget the events of September 11th, a turning point for America—and the world.

c. 1988	The terrorist organization known as al Qaeda forms in Afghanistan.
February 26, 1993	Terrorists set off a bomb in the parking garage of the World Trade Center. The blast kills 6 and injures 1,042.
February 23, 1998	Osama bin Laden issues a public declaration of war against the U.S.
August 7, 1998	Al Qaeda bombs U.S. embassies in Kenya and Tanzania, killing 224 and injuring more than 4,500.
October 12, 2000	Terrorists target the USS *Cole* at a Yemeni port, killing 17 sailors.
September 11, 2001	Hijackers crash four planes into the World Trade Center, the Pentagon, and a Pennsylvania field.
September 20, 2001	President George W. Bush declares a global War on Terror.
October 7, 2001	A U.S.-led coalition invades Afghanistan as part of Operation Enduring Freedom.
October 8, 2001	President Bush issues an executive order creating the Office of Homeland Security. It is restructured as the U.S. Department of Homeland Security in November 2002.
October 26, 2001	President Bush signs into law the USA PATRIOT Act.
November 19, 2001	Congress enacts the Aviation and Transportation Security Act, creating the Transportation Safety Administration (TSA).
January 2002	The Guantánamo Bay detention camp opens at the Guantánamo Bay Naval Base in Cuba.
May 28, 2002	Cleanup at Ground Zero officially ends.
March 20, 2003	A U.S.-led coalition invades Iraq as part of Operation Iraqi Freedom.
July 22, 2004	The 9/11 Commission releases its final report on the terror attacks.
May 1–2, 2011	Osama bin Laden is killed by U.S. Navy SEAL Team Six in Abbottabad, Pakistan.

atheists—people who do not believe in God or gods

Axis of Evil—the term used by the Bush administration to describe Iran, Iraq, and North Korea; the countries were accused of having weapons of mass destruction and links to terrorism

biological attacks—the intentional releases of poisons or disease-causing agents to harm living things

coalition—an alliance or partnership of groups or countries

communist—involving a system of government in which all property and business is owned and controlled by the state, with the goal of creating a classless society

conspiring—making a secret plan

cyberterrorism—a form of terrorism that uses computers, the Internet, and other technology to harm others

dictator—a ruler with complete power, who often rules by force

economic—having to do with money or business

extremism—the belief in using violence or other extreme measures to enforce uncompromising views

fundamentalist—an attitude that is based on strict religious beliefs

North Atlantic Treaty Organization (NATO)—a military alliance among the U.S., Canada, and several European nations

Pentagon—the headquarters of the U.S. Department of Defense in Washington, D.C.; the five-story building is made up of concentric, five-sided rings

pilgrimage—a religious journey made to a holy place; all Muslims who are able must make a pilgrimage to Mecca (in present-day Saudi Arabia) once in their lives

Port Authority of New York and New Jersey—the group that manages transportation systems in the New York–Newark metro area; its headquarters was based in the north tower of the World Trade Center

preemptive—describing something that is done as a preventive measure

primary—a special election in which voters choose among candidates from the same political party to run in a general election against candidates from other political parties

resistance—an organization or underground movement working against an opposition force

Saddam Hussein—(1937–2006) president of Iraq known as a brutal dictator who instigated conflicts such as the Iraq–Kuwait War; he was deposed in 2003 by a U.S.-led coalition and later sentenced to death

sharia—religious law based on the Koran and teachings of Muhammad that guides Islamic life; under sharia law, there is no separation of church and state

ultimatum—a demand that if rejected will result in consequences

"The 9/11 Tapes: The Story in the Air." *International New York Times*, September 7, 2011. http://www.nytimes.com/interactive/2011/09/08/nyregion/911-tapes.html?_r=0.

Bodden, Valerie. *The 9/11 Terror Attacks*. Mankato, Minn.: Creative Education, 2008.

Internet Archive. "September 11 Television Archive." https://archive.org/details/sept_11_tv_archive.

Langley, Andrew. *September 11: Attack on America*. Minneapolis: Compass Point Books, 2006.

Magnum Photographers. *New York September 11*. New York: PowerHouse Books, 2001.

National Commission on Terrorist Attacks upon the United States. *The 9/11 Commission Report*. New York: Norton, 2004.

One Nation: America Remembers September 11, 2001. Boston: Little, Brown, 2001.

Schier, Helga. *September 11, 2001*. Edina, Minn.: Abdo, 2008.

Wright, Lawrence. *The Looming Tower: Al-Qaeda and the Road to 9/11*. New York: Alfred A. Knopf, 2006.

9/11 Tribute Center: Online Story Collection
http://tributewtc.org/exhibits/online-story-collections
This site features videos, photos, and personal stories
from some of those affected by 9/11.

Scholastic: America Remembers 9/11
http://magazines.scholastic.com/news/2014/09/America-Remembers-9-11
Articles, videos, and a map accompany the experiences of kids on 9/11.

Note: Every effort has been made to ensure that the websites listed above are suitable for children, that they have educational value, and that they contain no inappropriate material. However, because of the nature of the Internet, it is impossible to guarantee that these sites will remain active indefinitely or that their contents will not be altered.

INDEX

7